## LAY BY

Lay By is a sensational play, written collectively by seven of Britain's leading young playwrights, inspired by a case of rape and indecent assault for which a man was convicted, perhaps unjustly, and sentenced to eight years' jail. It deals with the sub-culture of pornography as a whole and its effects on the people who practise, peddle and consume it; and in particular with the inadequacies of the law in dealing with ambivalent sexual situations like fellatio and flagellation.

The Royal Court Theatre, who originally commissioned the work, turned it down eventually. Its power and shock effect in performance cannot be over-rated and, when it was first presented at the 1971 Edinburgh Festival, it created ripples of disturbance, excitement and controversy. The critics were sharply divided in their reactions, even on the same paper, Nicholas de Jongh of The Guardian hailing it as a major theatrical breakthrough while his colleague Michael Billington condemned it. It was later seen at The Royal Court Theatre, for Sunday night performances only, and at The Open Space Theatre, London, for a short season. Despite the many hands in its creation, the play has an amazingly taut stylistic unity, which makes it as effective to read as to see.

The various authors have all made their mark as writers in the theatre. Howard Brenton is the author of several plays performed on the fringe and elsewhere, including the award-winning Christie in Love: Brian Clark is well known in theatre-in-education circles and has written several television plays: Trevor Griffiths is the author of the much-acclaimed Occupations (Playscript 62) which was presented by the Royal Shakespeare Company and Sam Sam, at the Open Space Theatre: David Hare wrote the award-winning Slag, and The Great Exhibition (recently presented at The Hampstead Theatre Club, London): Stephen Poliakoff has had plays presented at The Traverse Theatre Club, Edinburgh: Hugh Stoddart is currently resident playwright at The Greenwich Theatre, London: and Snoo Wilson is the author of Pignight (presented at The Young Vic, London) and Blow Job (presented at The King's Head Theatre Club, London, by The Portable Theatre Company).

# PLAYSCRIPT 66

Howard Brenton
Brian Clark
Trevor Griffiths
David Hare

Stephen
 Poliakoff
Hugh Stoddart
Snoo Wilson

BY

CALDER AND BOYARS · LONDON

First published in Great Britain  1972
by Calder & Boyars Ltd
18 Brewer Street London W1

ISBN 0 7145 0928 0  Cloth Edition
ISBN 0 7145 0929 9  Paper Edition

Printed in Great Britain by
Biddles Ltd
Guildford, Surrey

# LAY BY

LAY BY was first performed as a joint Portable Theatre and Traverse Theatre Club production at The Traverse Theatre Club, Edinburgh, during the Edinburgh Festival, on August 24th, 1971, with the following cast:

| | |
|---|---|
| PORNOGRAPHER, JACK | James Warrior |
| JOY, MARGE, MAUREEN | Meg Davies |
| DADDY, BARBER, DICK, POLICEMAN | Mark York |
| DUMMY, POLICEMAN, DOUG | Graham Simpson |
| LESLEY | Catherine Kessler |
| DOCTOR | Nicholas Nacht |

The play was directed by Snoo Wilson

(At the back of the stage there is a cut out drawing of a van. Crude, black and white. The windscreen is wide enough to accommodate three people abreast. All the other windows are blank. Lights up. Two actors playing a VENTRILOQUIST and his DUMMY)

DUMMY. Daddy? What did they do in the field?

DADDY. I told you that.

DUMMY. Tell me again. I like to hear you tell me, 'bout what the man and the ladies did in the field.

DADDY. Well, son, this is the story. They were in the field...

DUMMY. Were they farmers, Daddy?

DADDY. Not exactly.

DUMMY. Picnic, picnic, was it a picnic?

DADDY. A kind of picnic, son.

DUMMY. What did they eat, daddy, what did they eat, did they eat nice things like... jam?

DADDY. They didn't eat anything.

DUMMY. Sounds a rotten picnic. I said sounds a rotten picnic. If they didn't eat anything.

DADDY. Now sonny, do you want to hear the story or don't you?

7

DUMMY. Oh yes yes yes!

DADDY. Well you see... Are you ready?

DUMMY. Yes yes!

(DUMMY fidgeting violently rubbing his buttocks on his DAD's knees)

DADDY. Then I'll begin.

DUMMY. What's a story called what's a story called?

DADDY. The story is called

(Pause)

A man, and a woman, he a bit sharp, dubious, she a forty year old school teacher with five kids, divorced from her soldier husband, who has deserted her for foreign parts, drive their van along up the M4 diverting to the A4 just before Maidenhead. His head all kinds of flash ideas, in her head God knows what, perhaps five kids and the soldier husband, who has deserted her for foreign parts, stops the van, to the sexy little thumb of an eighteen year old girl, or, was she forced into the van by the point of a knife, or not, he puts his hand between her legs, for he says she opened them, she says he never touched her, the van turns off the road, and stops, the man climbs into the back of the van with the girl or the girl is forced into the back of the van by a knife point, the girl undresses, or is forced to undress, the man rubs contraceptive cream on her cunt, and intercourse takes place, but without emission, the girl then takes the man's penis into her mouth, under duress she says, he says voluntarily, the man ejaculates, she swallows says the man, she spits it out says the girl, the man produces a cane kept normally for use on the dog, says the man, he thrashes the girl's buttocks with the cane, kept normally for use on the dog, and all this time the other woman, forty year old schoolteacher divorced from her soldier husband, who has deserted her for foreign parts, looks on, or averts her eyes, and the man and the older woman drive off into the future of

8

DUMMY: Graham Simpson.          DADDY: Mark York.

DADDY.  ...His head all kinds of flash ideas, in her head
    God knows what...

endless and endless discovery and revelation.

(Pause)

DUMMY. Eergh.

(They exit, the VENTRILOQUIST guiding the DUMMY.
Enter the PORNOGRAPHER immediately. He carries a
camera and tripod. He has a hunchback. He is dressed
in a three piece suit)

PORNOGRAPHER. A lovely sunny day. Nature on the go
everywhere. Bunnies popping out of hedgerows, licking
each other's ears. Field mice tickling one another's
little behinds. In the ditches sticklebacks having it off
with their own tails. On each blade of grass grasshoppers
belting their legs together like a million modern jazz
combos. And up above in the air, birds, blackbirds,
starlings, larks outwarbling Buddy Holly. Ah, all things
bright and beautiful.

(Calls off)

Over here girls. Mind the cowpats.

(JOY and LESLEY enter. JOY is dressed in C & A
hotpants outfit. LESLEY is dressed in jeans and T
shirt with long sleeves. They carry a table in between
them. It has one blanket on it)

LESLEY. I'm all sticky.

JOY. You might have helped. Unloading the van.

LESLEY. All sticky underneath.

PORNOGRAPHER. Had to find a field, didn't I? Had to
find a site, suitably artistic. (Looks round with his
viewfinder) A garish venue.

LESLEY. Come on.

PORNOGRAPHER. Ah. Yes. Right my darlings. (Finally
chooses a spot) There.

(He looks at the scene with one hand over his eye. The
GIRLS totter over to where he wants)

LESLEY. I'm so sticky. Like sweating glue. Oh I'd love a
swim.

PORNOGRAPHER. Sorry, nasty shadow. Let's see what we
come up with...

(Looks hard at one place, then points at another)

Here. Yes. Get the pink edges against the dark
mysterious luxuriance of that hedge. Really sharp.

LESLEY. If there's a lake around, we could have a swim.
I'd like a swim. Be lovely and cool.

(They move the bed again)

JOY. Poncing about.

PORNOGRAPHER. Oh no!

JOY. What?

PORNOGRAPHER. That won't do. I mean, the image is all
wrong. Fucking great silage tower stuck in the middle
foreground for a start. Look at it. (Gestures) I mean.
(Wipes his brow) Can't have sexy photos of frolics in
the countryside with a fucking great silage tower stuck in
the middle foreground. Destroys the whole... phantasma
of the fantasy.

JOY. Field. Bed. Dolly on the bed. In the field. That's
what the man wanted in 'it? And then get back to
London. (To LESLEY) Get your knickers off. (Looks round
suspiciously) I don't like the countryside. It's not...
natural.

PORNOGRAPHER. What d'you mean? How can nature be not
natural?

JOY. I don't like it. It's not... indoors.

LESLEY. There's a lake over there. Shall we have a swim?

PORNOGRAPHER. (annoyed) What? What lake?

LESLEY. Get the sweat off. Make me look better in the photograph. Without sweat.

PORNOGRAPHER. What lake? I can't see no lake.

LESLEY. I can hold my breath under water for two minutes. Nearly.

PORNOGRAPHER. That's no lake. That's light off the tin roof of the barn. The glare, an optical effect -

LESLEY. It's not.

PORNOGRAPHER. It's a mirage.

LESLEY. Look, there are swans.

PORNOGRAPHER. Seagulls, you little twerp. Oh you little twerp, you cheap little smutty... Seagulls. Perching on the tin roof. Get it? Heat haze, like a lens. It's a distortion.

LESLEY. It's a lake.

PORNOGRAPHER. Thick aren't you? Nipple brained.

(LESLEY looks at him. Then turns away)

LESLEY. Come on Joy, let's have a swim.

PORNOGRAPHER. You've not heard a word I've said, have you? A day in the life of a pornographic photographer. Wow, zap, boom, shazzam, ker-pow, way out, groove, it's all here.

(He sets up the tripod. LESLEY changes into black negligée)

Right my dear, give us the double grocer. Hurry up, I haven't got all day.

(LESLEY climbs on the table)

LESLEY. Just a minute.

PORNOGRAPHER. Squeeze it.

(She squeezes her breasts at him)

LESLEY. No give us a mo - I had this idea.

PORNOGRAPHER. Call that squeezing? My old mother
    could do better...

LESLEY. It's goin' to hurt. (Pause) It does.

PORNOGRAPHER. More over the top. And behind. No,
    too far. Right, right. (Another pose) Now get set up.
    I'll be wanting the split beaver. (Nasty) If it's not too
    much trouble.

(LESLEY poses)

LESLEY. Monday. Breakfast coke and aspirin. Eleven
    o'clock two benzedrine. After a hard weekend one
    mandrax. Benzedrine takes you too high. Mandrax
    brings you down. Bender and chips. Knickerbocker
    glory. Black bomber Kingston-by-pass.

PORNOGRAPHER. Cross-buttock. Colour. Poke it at me,
    love.

(Changes pose)

LESLEY. Tuesday, Bluesday. Bad. Stelazine. Got the
    shakes. Need for disipal. Battered sausages and chips.
    M4.

PORNOGRAPHER. And now good news. It's the Lustful Turk.
    Dildo. For me it's the telephoto. This one for the back
    room displays, my love.

(Changes pose)

LESLEY. Wednesday. Ether for B. Kelloggs and condensed

LESLEY: Catherine Kessler.

LESLEY. No drapes.

milk. Speed through to Thursday. M40 to Gloucester.

PORNOGRAPHER. Greek urn.

LESLEY. No drapes.

PORNOGRAPHER. Right - Roman urn.

LESLEY. No 'elmet.

PORNOGRAPHER. All right. Just come at me, come on now. Come on.

LESLEY. Then Friday. Hot bath with Librium. Tincture of cannabis on Woodies. Squirt of French fern. Song of Norway at Weybridge ABC. Raspberry Bigtime Tub. Mandrax. Really, don't like the road. Garage in Hendon.

(Blackout. Strobe on, one-second intervals. She slowly takes off negligee, the PORNOGRAPHER circles her and she keeps turning. At each flash a different position for each of them)

PORNOGRAPHER. Right. Feel free. Let it come. Right over the top. Digital entry. Niggerlips. Stormtrooper. The thongs. In the irons. Milkman calls. Dying Gaul. The Governess. The Slave unashamed. Sermon on the Mount. The Berlin Wall. The Iron Virgin. Song of Norway. Leg up. Arm up. Leg over. Hold your tits together. Let them go. Smile.

(The strobe stops. Lights up. LESLEY gets dressed)

LESLEY. Saturday. Bag of crisps and a Pepsi. A4. Back of the van. I let this fella fuck me. I sucked him off.

PORNOGRAPHER. Lovely.

LESLEY. I sucked him off.

(PORNOGRAPHER lies on the table, shuts his eyes)

PORNOGRAPHER. Lovely sunny day.

15

LESLEY. And then the dirty bugger goes and rapes me.

(Exit. Pause. Enter JOY)

JOY. You'll get sunstroke lying there.

PORNOGRAPHER. You back? Where's the other?

JOY. She's all right.

PORNOGRAPHER. I'm sure she's all right. Where is she then?

JOY. She's comin'.

PORNOGRAPHER. What did you do then?

JOY. I watched her.

PORNOGRAPHER. Story of your life. (She looks hard at him) It's a joke.

JOY. All right.

PORNOGRAPHER. Give 'er a shot. Time the meat was on the slab again.

(LESLEY walks on, bleeding from the knees and elbows)

What the hell have you been doing?

LESLEY. I've been for a swim.

PORNOGRAPHER. Joy, take her away and clean her up will you.

(JOY bustles LESLEY off. PORNOGRAPHER comes forward and gives out hardcore photos of gang-bangs, sodomy, fellatio etc.)

Just hand these out, will you?

(As the audience pass them round, he talks)

16

Now that's a good pic. Swedish. They're popular.
They got a lot going for them because of the Swedish
tag. They're cheap because they're produced legally
and so it doesn't have to be all hole and corner. The
customs get to recognise the parcels and bleed off
about fifteen per cent. It's a reasonable argument.
You talk to a customs officer and he's confused about
what to let through and what to hold back. That's if
he's straight. If he's wise he sees it's all public opinion
anyhow and wants his cut. Four thousand copies of
Split Beaver weekly isn't going to do much for anyone
if it's burned. Mostly it's magazines they export but
occasionally there's a big consignment of photos. Thing
about magazines is they got a good resale value
if they're well bound - but you need a decent electro
copier, binding machinery, four colour press. It's too
bulky for this country. The cops find out where it's all
coming from and they'll smash it up likely as not.
You're hardly in a position to complain.

(Pause)

I use a Leica, and a cheap Japanese twinlens reflex.
I got an Arriflex enlarger which I got off a fence and an
Ilfoprint machine. That's when you buy paper that's
been impregnated with developer and it goes through a
bath in about ten seconds. You don't even have to fix
them. I have a Paterson wash tank with through flow
disturbed water and capacity for a hundred twelve by
fifteen. If anyone comes, I'm just an amateur. It's
very difficult to prove sales. All the equipment is
insured so I can start again if it gets broken up. Most
of the day I'm a broker. I do this stuff generally only for
specific commission. It's not remunerative to flog them
yourself. You'd get your mug known for a start. There's
a bloke in Acton who uses his front room in the evenings.
He hasn't changed the fittings in ten years. (Pause) The
Acton photographer. Yeah. I don't know how some of his
stuff gets sold at all. He paints out the genital organs.
He shakes the fucking camera. He don't have the first
idea of how to use a light meter. He's just not using
what he's got. Some of the blokes, sometimes, they
haven't been able to get a hardon in front of the camera.
Then the Acton photographer has a tendency to move in

PORNOGRAPHER: James Warrior.

PORNOGRAPHER. The cops find out where it's all coming from and they'll smash it up likely as not.

too close. Smegma all over the lens. (Pause) The thing
about good photos is they're usually commissioned by
collectors. Not like the stuff passed round the building
site in a tea break. But it's a dying trade. Lonely man's
hobby. All these get-together clubs, lonely hearts,
computerdating, I reckon it's spoiling the market. These
couples get together with their super eight film cameras
and zoom in on each other's privates. They don't like
the anonymity any more. It has to be someone they know.
Uncle Bill, Aunt Maud or Marilyn Monroe. Sometimes I
get called in to do a romp. I don't join in. Can't mix
business and pleasure. (Pause) I like it with two or three.
It's more social. I don't see what's up with people
actually. The whole thing is stupid. Going round with a
piece of flesh that you could be arrested for showing. I
mean, we all know what it looks like. It's art that
makes it interesting.

(He gathers the pictures in)

Now if you'd be so kind to pass them back.

(He takes them back. Re-enter LESLEY and JOY.
PORNOGRAPHER sets up tripod near the table)

Anyone would think that you were enjoying this. (Pause)
I mean anyone would think that you weren't paid to do
this, that a nice afternoon in the country is just what
you've been thirsting for all week. (Pause) Fucking hell.
Look five quid. I said five quid. For an afternoon.

(He lies down and takes off his trousers and pants)

LESLEY. How much do you get for those snaps?

PORNOGRAPHER. I barely cover my overheads. I said, I'm
struggling. (Emphatic) I've got to get these photos. They
got to be good or there's no sale. This is important to
me. It matters. Lots of pussy in the sun. I know it's a
drowsy day, I'm seeing pondlife in front of my eyes,
but work comes first. You got to keep it on the go. We'll
have an oral. I want you to watch. (Positions her) That's
lovely. Look stern. School mistress. That's right.
You ought to have a cane. Never mind. Now come down

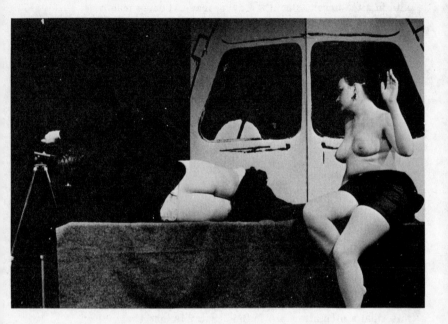

PORNOGRAPHER: James Warrior.    MAUREEN: Meg Davies.

PORNOGRAPHER.  I barely cover my overheads.  I said,
    I'm struggling.

on me. (He puts the camera within reach. LESLEY is doing something in his crutch)

LESLEY. Can't you do better than that?

PORNOGRAPHER. Must be something to do with the sun. Sunstroke. Roll it between your palms. That usually does the trick. Joy. Start taking your clothes off. That's lovely, Lesley, I can feel it coming up a treat. Joy, can you look a bit sharper, nastier. (Pause) Beautiful. Don't step back. Head up a moment, Lesley. (Click) Grab it. (Click) Hold it (Click) Stare at it. Kiss it. (Click)

LESLEY. It's not going to come, is it?

PORNOGRAPHER. Nowhere near. (Pause) That's lovely Joy. Get out the knife. It opens with that little button at the side. Come up off me Lesley. Head up. You're exhausted now. Droop of the eyes. Buttocks to camera. Beseech. Mouth open. They'll love this. Trace of moisture on the lower lip. (Click) Mouth open. (Pause) Joy, stop pissing around and keep looking.

JOY. There's a bull doing it with a cow in the next field.

(Exits)

PORNOGRAPHER. Oh yes. Eyes shut, Lesley. Hands out. As in prayer. They'll love this, they'll really love this.

(Slow fade to blackout as they get dressed. LESLEY hums the Wimpy song, off key. In the blackout, LESLEY and her friend MAUREEN sing)

LESLEY & MAUREEN.
Setting the trends
Each day ends
Like the last
Hitting the heights
The bright lights
Going so fast.

(The lights go up. LESLEY and MAUREEN sit on the

21

table facing the audience. BARBER, a well dressed
investigator, sits to one side. He pays close attention
to the girls' words. Occasionally he notes a phrase)

Why should we worry before we get old?
Why should we do what we're told?
It's a Wimpyful world out there.

LESLEY. This tomato's blocked.

(They laugh)

MAUREEN. You know this bloke I been going with?

LESLEY. You mean Kirk Douglas?

MAUREEN. Yeah. Him. Wanna know what we did last
night?

LESLEY. No?

MAUREEN. I wish you could of seen us. He said he'd
take me to see his ancestors. I wish you could of seen
us. I said where d'you keep 'em? Know where we
went? Up the cemetery. He had a bottle of Bourbon
whisky. It was nice. The moon. We sat by a tree. He
was nice. He held off. We looked for his ancestors but
we couldn't find 'em. His mother had cancer. One of
his ancestors was a pirate. We finished the whisky and
he held me hand on the way back.

LESLEY. I was fucked last night.

MAUREEN. Oh yes.

LESLEY. Yes.

MAUREEN. Up the base?

LESLEY. I was hitching back from the caff.

MAUREEN. Oh. (Pause) What did he have?

LESLEY. A van.

22

MAUREEN. Oh. What was he?

LESLEY. He was in carpets. He had a van. Clean.

MAUREEN. Bumpy.

LESLEY. He had a mattress...but it hurt. It still hurts.

MAUREEN. Rough.

LESLEY. No - he used the jelly.

MAUREEN. Unsafe.

LESLEY. No no. He withdrew.

MAUREEN. One of those. Think you're a wastepaper
   basket.

LESLEY. No. He come in my mouth.

MAUREEN. (excited) That's disgusting.

LESLEY. It's all right.

MAUREEN. Lesley.

LESLEY. Do you like that?

MAUREEN. It's all right. Seeing him again?

LESLEY. No.

MAUREEN. Why not? If you like it?

LESLEY. It hurt.

MAUREEN. Suckin' doesn't hurt. Does it?

LESLEY. It wasn't suckin'.

MAUREEN. More than suckin'?

LESLEY. Sort of.

MAUREEN. What d'you mean?

LESLEY. He hit me.

MAUREEN. That all?

LESLEY. With a dog whip.

MAUREEN. He whipped you?

LESLEY. Yeah.

MAUREEN. What did you do?

LESLEY. Well I - (Lost for words)

MAUREEN. What did you do?

LESLEY. I - dunno. I was on speed. I dunno.

MAUREEN. Oh Lesley, really.

(MAUREEN exits in a huff. Music cue. 15 seconds of
bonzo dog band, "In the canyons of your mind". Quick
fade. LESLEY picks up a copy of "Lover" and starts to
read it)

LESLEY. June felt a searing white explosion as Bob
kissed her. Suddenly it all made sense. He held her
tightly and she could feel him move inside his nylon
rolltop. Come down to the beach, he breathed, almost
without moving his lips. And Lesley wordlessly walked
off the verandah and followed him, the night wind blowing
her soft blonde tresses over her brown shoulder still
warm from a lazy afternoon on a hot beach where Pierrot
a fisherman had offered to take them out in his boat.
You'd better watch that Pierrot. No no said Lesley, he
saved my life once when the tide...

(She puts it down, bored. BARBER comes over and
removes it, primly puts it in his briefcase. Pause)

My mum said she'd turn me out when she found me
doing it for money. S'alright if you've got it, it's if

you haven't got it. If there weren't blokes wanting it I
wouldn't have to do it. I didn't go much to school. I
used to ring up and say I was sick. Me and my friends
left at fifteen and we went to work in the Sterling Cable
factory down the A4. Four bob an hour, it's fucking
murder. You think I come when I suck off? I don't think
about nothing when I do it. The welfare officer told
my Mum it's because I'm not secure. Eight rotten quid
a week I got at the caff. Course I'm not secure. They
found I was going with the drivers round the back. They
sacked me after the Health Inspector called. Said I was
spreading clap all over the South of England. It
radiated out from me in little circles. The police had
a map they said, marking the spread. The welfare
told my Mum I was an underachiever, but they never
caught me with purple hearts and that. The police
they're scared to search you properly, even the ladies.
I started taking meth when someone at school gave me
one for a suck. I have to take ever such a lot now and
it's getting more expensive. That and you can't get
Mandrax any more. If you can stay awake Mandrax is
great. Makes you feel nothing matters. I don't see
what's wrong with it. I mean, speed is like booze. It's
all the same. Speed makes me want to talk. I make
lots of plans on speed. It's tough when you can't get
any and have to go back on aspirin and cider. I don't
like booze. I knew this bloke, a wino. He pisses blood.
And he don't ever eat properly. The welfare said I
don't eat properly, so I got spots and that. It's not a
dose, I don't think. I saw this book on VD. I didn't read
it though. I don't expect I'll live very long. I'd like to
die like Jayne Mansfield. There was a mini went under
the tail of a big lorry outside the caff. There were
bits everywhere. The fire brigade ran a hose out from
the kitchens and hosed down the road.

(She lies down on the table. In a childish voice:)

When I grow up I'm going to have a frying pan...a
settee...and a house...and doilies...and babies...and
a vacuum cleaner and knives and forks...and children...
and they'd better be good or I'll smack them...and if
they show their wee-wees I'll lock them in a cupboard
with...dead rats and potties I'll have three bunny jelly

moulds...lots and lots of buttons and a telephone to
ring up the grocer like Mrs. McGreedy. (She sits up
again) I used to crunch up methadone and inject it with
H. It makes your veins go funny, all sort of septic.
When I had my abortion the doctors wanted to put me
under with an injection but they couldn't find a decent
vein. I had one but I was buggered if they were going to
queer that one too.

(Pause. Brings chair forward)

BARBER. (sympathetic) Lesley, don't you think it's
possible that you've been misled?

LESLEY. The inside of my nose is full of cornflakes.

(She laughs helplessly)

BARBER. Lesley -

LESLEY. I got this terrific idea to set up cornflake
stalls all up and down the A4 supplied by - my nose.
Maybe you'd like to join in.

BARBER. Did you consent to fellatio? Were you raped?
Can you say anything about the contraceptive cream and
how he used it? Who did you tell first?

LESLEY. (fantasy ending) I told Maureen...then I told
Mum... Then Mum rang up and I told the police.

BARBER. Were you raped?

LESLEY. (annoyed) Course I was raped. My arse is sore.

BARBER. It is penetration without consent that is rape in
the law. Not indecent assault. When he beat you it was
indecent assault.

LESLEY. It was rape. Course it was. I mean rape is
indecent assault. He indecently assaulted me.

BARBER. Can we go through the evening again? Start at
the beginning.

26

LESLEY. (dully) My mother always used to tell me that I ought to save myself for the right man. About midnight on May 27th 1970 I was walking from a caff in Theale to my home in Woolhamton eight miles away. Passing Mac's caff I was approached by the van in question. I didn't go much to school. I went to work in Sterling Cable. The welfare told my Mum I was an underachiever. Lesley felt a searing white hot explosion as Bob kissed her. Suddenly it all made sense.

(She goes and stands behind the windscreen of the van)

JACK. (goes to driving position in windscreen) About midnight on May 27th I picked up a girl who was hitching by the side of the road. I drove on. I started fondling her legs and when she parted them I assumed she would be willing to have sexual intercourse.

LESLEY. Mainlined meth half an hour ago. Stoned out of my mind.

JACK. I stopped the van in a lay-by. I climbed into the back with Lesley. There was a mattress. She consented. Consent is essential to my pleasure.

(They disappear out of sight into the back of the van with MRS. X, MARGE, left visible in the front seat powdering her nose)

MARGE. Here. Jack. Do you think you could take me home first?

JACK. Later. In a minute. There's plenty time.

LESLEY. (whispers) You will be careful, won't you? I don't want to have a baby.

JACK. (whispers) It's all right. I've got some jelly.

(Long pause. MARGE continues powdering her nose. Squeaking of mattress. Stop. Pause)

MARGE. Have you done?

JACK. (whispers) It'd be safer for you if I didn't come inside you.

LESLEY. What d'you mean?

JACK. Are you experienced?

LESLEY. What you mean?

JACK. You had oral experience?

LESLEY. What?

JACK. The mouth.

LESLEY. Go on. Course you can kiss me.

JACK. No no no no no. Suck my cock.

LESLEY. All right. (Pause)

JACK. You got lovely teeth. All right is it? Clean?

LESLEY. Glynmph.

JACK. Not so hard. That's lovely. (Speaks normally) Hey. Marge. Have a look at this. You're no novice. I'll say she's no novice!

MARGE. Jack, did you clean up that oil in the corner?

JACK. (panting) Course I did. Look, for Christ's sake, look.

MARGE. (resumes powdering her nose) Well, I was only worried in case you got your jacket soiled.

JACK. For Christ's sake turn round.

(You see his hand appear and grab MARGE by the shoulder to get her attention)

MARGE. Well I was just worried. You go ahead and enjoy yourself.

JACK. (pulling at MARGE with one hand) Don't stop now.

LESLEY. (muffled) Give us a chance.

JACK. Come on. Turkish delight. Storm trooper. The
thongs. The Governess. The milkman calls. Greek urn.
Niggerlips. F.8. Split beaver. Song of Norway.
Naughty schoolgirl. Look at me, Marge. Jesus look at
me. Tights pantees boots suspenders nipples - will you
fucking look at me - black gloves wet nylon nighty.
Suck suck suck suck. Aaah. (He comes. Pause. MARGE
lights a cigarette)

MARGE. After my husband left me I took up with Jack...
He's careful. I mean, he wouldn't knock you up. He
always uses French protectives. I don't think there's
anything more wrong than bringing unwanted babies
into the world. My husband got me pregnant five times
in a row and then he left me. It's hard on the kids.You've
got to have money to look after them. Jack's ever so
generous when he's got it. He told me right out he was
kinky, but what's kinky? Babies don't grow in your
mouth. When my husband was drunk he's hit me on the
face if I said I wasn't ready for him. It hurt. No jelly.
No love. Just another baby.

(Pause. A whipping noise)

LESLEY. Here, what's that?

JACK. Wouldn't you like this?

(Whap whap)

LESLEY. Here

(WHAP WHAP)

What you doing?

JACK. Don't you like it?

(WHAP WHAP)

29

LESLEY. No, lay off...stop it... (Screams) Stop it...
stop, stop.

JACK. Oh all right. Some people like it. Discipline.

LESLEY. Well I don't.

JACK. All right, love. No harm done.

LESLEY. Well, there is to my bum. It stings.

JACK. Bit of a tingle.

LESLEY. It hurts.

JACK. You'll be all right. I thought you'd like it. I like
it.

LESLEY. Well it wasn't you who was getting it.

JACK. All right love. You want to come back with us for a
cup of tea.

LESLEY. No, I'm going home.

JACK. We'll take you home then.

LESLEY. I've had enough of you. I'm off.

(She scrambles out of the back of the van adjusting her
dress)

JACK. (hurt) See you round then.

(LESLEY stands downstage)

MARGE. You shouldn't have used that cane.

JACK. Thought she'd like it.

MARGE. You want to be more careful.

JACK. No harm done.

MARGE.
One I love
Two I loathe
Three I cast away
Four I love with all my heart
Five I love I say
Six he loves me
Seven he don't
Eight he'll marry me
Nine he won't
Ten he would if he could but he can't
Eleven he comes
Twelve he tarries
Thirteen he's waiting
Fourteen he marries

(JACK and MARGE come out and stand in front of the van together. LESLEY facing them other side of the stage. BARBER in the middle)

BARBER. I see.

(Long thoughtful pause)

There's really nothing to be afraid of, is there, Lesley?

LESLEY. (shrugs)

BARBER. Is there, Lesley? There's nothing, nothing at all to be afraid of?

LESLEY. No.

BARBER. It would help if you would answer the questions as clearly and as promptly as you are able. Justice may well depend on it. We seek the truth. Clean, clear, objective, rational. (Breaking it down) In other words, we wish to establish...find out...what happened on the night of May 27th, 1970, in the back of the older of the two vans owned at the time by the man you see facing you. (Pause) I asked whether you saw anything to be afraid of in that.

31

LESLEY. (low) No.

BARBER. Again.

LESLEY. No.

BARBER. Good. We progress. We progress. As we must
progress. Progress. Inch by inch. Tooth by nail.
Gibbon, Goebbels. We keep our tiny purchase on the
lonely rockface of betterment. Not long ago we hanged
a child for stealing sheep. We branded and tortured
for merest misdemeanour. Chains and the pillory. Men
broken on the wheel of their belief. And below us
always, deeper and darker as we claw our way upwards,
the great black pit of past barbarism, cant and prejudice.
But. We. Progress. Let me try to get it right, Lesley.
That, after all, is my job. It's what...I do best. You
have claimed that the man...Jack there...and his...
accomplice...constrained you to come...

LESLEY. What's that?

BARBER. What is what?

LESLEY. What's constrained?

BARBER. Made.

LESLEY. Eh?

BARBER. Forced.

LESLEY. Oh, yeah.

BARBER. It is your word, Lesley.

LESLEY. No, I don' think so.

BARBER. (flourish) Let me... (Fiddles with papers from
his briefcase) refresh your memory a little. I read
from your statement at the police station. May 28th.
The day after... (Mumbling, reading) Here we are...
"Then the two of them constrained me to perform the
above act." Your statement. Your words. Mmm?

32

LESLEY. Well. He did.

BARBER. So you claim. Well then, Lesley. You still
claim that...the two accused constrained you to perform
the act of fellatio.

LESLEY. Is that in the... (Points to mouth. BARBER nods)
That's right.

BARBER. I see. How?

LESLEY. What?

BARBER. How?

LESLEY. (finger in mouth) Yike yat.

BARBER. No...how did they force you to do it?

LESLEY. I don't know how you mean.

BARBER. Did he threaten you?

LESLEY. Yeah.

BARBER. What with?

LESLEY. Oh you know. All sorts.

BARBER. Ahuh. What sort of all sorts?

LESLEY. He said he'd hit me. And she had a knife.

BARBER. Really. Did you see the knife?

LESLEY. Yeah. Was on her lap.

BARBER. And you were where?

LESLEY. I was in the back, wan' I?

BARBER. But you saw a knife in the lap of that woman,
who was sitting in the front seat.

LESLEY. Yeah.

(BARBER takes a dildo from his inside pocket and walks over to JACK. Straps it on with meticulous and wholly absorbed care. Stands. Looks at it. Turns)

BARBER. What d'you call one of those, Lesley?

LESLEY. It's a dildo, innit.

BARBER. Yes. I meant, what portion of the male anatomy does it represent?

LESLEY. Well, it's his thing.

BARBER. Thank you. The truth does not need to be whispered, my dear. So, you would normally refer to a man's member as his...thing. Is that right?

LESLEY. I s'pose so.

BARBER. You suppose so? Don't you know?

LESLEY. Yeah. All right. It's his thing.

BARBER. It's important we get this right. I want to use your words. Your own words. The words that come quite naturally to you. (Pause) His - thing. Very well. I'd like you now to perform a very simple re-enactment of the moment at which fellatio occurred.

LESLEY. Here, I'm not...

BARBER. There is nothing to be afraid of, remember. (Holds arm out. She walks hesitantly forward. He crosses her in front of him) Now, perhaps you will be good enough to take up your positions.

(JACK kneels down, thighs splayed, dildo semi-couchant. MARGE stands, her back to his. LESLEY kneels face within inches of the dildo)

Good. Can you remember what Mr. Corker said, Lesley?

34

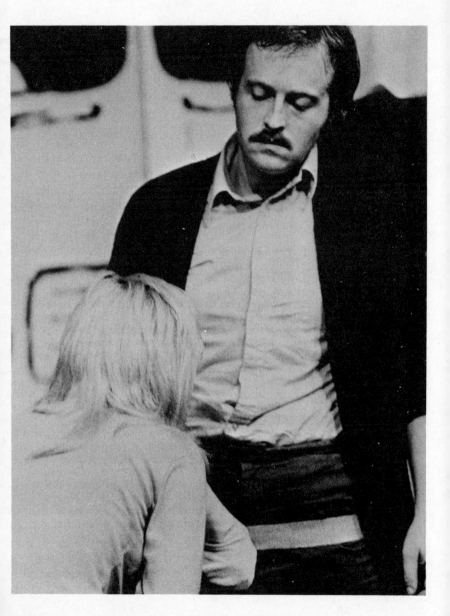

LESLEY: Catherine Kessler. JACK: James Warrior.

(JACK kneels down, thighs splayed, dildo semi-couchant...)

LESLEY. He said something like...

JACK. (sourly) Here you are.

BARBER. And you said?

LESLEY. I didn't say anything.

BARBER. You didn't protest? You didn't, for example, scream.

LESLEY. No. What for? I was in a van in a lay-by.

BARBER. What did you do?

LESLEY. I opened my mouth. Like that.

BARBER. Yes. (Waving the dildo in)

LESLEY. Ag e ck ii ike at.

BARBER. (getting down to study it. Walking round to the
    other side) Ahuh. (Finally) Now then, Lesley, perhaps
    you would tell the court who you consider to be in
    command of the situation at this precise moment. He
    has constrained you to take his thing...into your mouth.
    You have done so. Your lips and tongue and palate...and
    teeth...now rest upon his member. Mmm? Who would
    you say was in charge?

LESLEY. Ot?

BARBER. Wouldn't you say the accused was taking something
    of a risk? Mmm? Forcing someone wholly hostile to the
    idea to take his member in her mouth? I suppose you do
    realise that your jaws, an average pair of human jaws,
    can exert enough combined pressure to dent a piece of
    tempered steel. One thousand and forty two pounds of
    pressure, Lesley. Think of that. In your jaws. Try it.
    See for yourself.

LESLEY. Ot?

BARBER. Bite!

36

(She bites the dildo)

Bite!

(She bites harder. The glans penis comes off with a
tearing sound. JACK falls backwards slightly on his
heels. She spits it onto the floor. BARBER picks up the
pieces and drops them behind the van)

However. Jack Corker sentenced to 8 years for rape,
two years for indecent assault. His mistress, 3 years
for aiding and abetting. However.

(Blackout. The cast with the exception of MARGE, pick
up boards with a row of kids painted black on white in
the idiom of the van. With these in the next scene they
form circles and squares, alternately menacing MARGE
and retreating but almost always the boards face her)

KIDS. (skipping in a circle)
Miss is kind and Miss is gentle
Miss is strong and Miss is mental

(They repeat this three times, the light comes up, KIDS
turn to audience)

Ha ha ha.

(During this verse MARGE comes on with a whistle.
KIDS sing)

Teacher teacher the coppers are after thee
If they catch you they'll give you a month or three
They'll tie you up with wi-er
Behind the Black Mari-er
So get in the van
With your dirty old man
And head for the Irish Sea.

(MARGE comes on and blows the whistle. A horrible
pause. The children sing the above verse again, but
crowding round her. Now they don't sing it, they say
it)

KID: Catherine Kessler.

KIDS. (skipping in a circle)
    Miss is kind and Miss is gentle
    Miss is strong and Miss is mental

Teacher teacher the coppers are after thee
If they catch you they'll give you a month or three
They'll tie you up with wi-er
Behind the Black Mar-ier
So get in the van
With your dirty old man
And... Head... For... The... Irish... Sea.

(Silence)

MARGE. In time.

(Pause)

In time. The whistle's gone. (Blows the whistle again.
Silence. The KIDS don't move)

Straight lines.

(They don't move. She shouts shrilly)

In time! Straight lines! In time!

(Blows the whistle hard)

Whistle's gone, straight lines!

(Blows the whistle again)

1ST KID. 'Ere you hear summat?

(They cock their heads)

KIDS. Wot?

1ST KID. Could have sworn I heard summat.

2ND. Maybe it was the Concorde.

3RD. Or teacher farting.

KIDS. There was summat.

Wot?

Wot?

Wot?

MARGE. In time, in time, I said in time.

KIDS. (KIDS sing)
Same to you with knobs on
Cabbages with clogs on
Elephants with slippers on
And you with dirty knickers on.

(MARGE blows the whistle three times)

MARGE. I'll tell the headmistress. I'll tell her! About
all of you.

KIDS. (KIDS sing)
Oh...

Tell her smell her
Kick her down the cellar.

MARGE. Thirty seconds. Thirty seconds to get in line!

(KIDS stare her out)

I want a straight line in front of me.

(Pause. They stare)

It's your own time you're wasting!

(Pause. They stare)

If I tell the headmistress, she'll keep you all in.

(Pause. They stare)

It's no skin off my nose.

KIDS. (KIDS sing)
If you want to do some time
Ask a teacher

MARGE. (getting hysterical)

You little...bastards.

(KIDS recoil in mock shock)

KIDS.
Oh oh Miss
That hurt miss
What's a bastard, Miss?

Miss Miss what's a bastard?
Miss Miss.

MARGE. I'm going to, I am, I'm going to tell on you little
bastards.

1ST KID. (to another) I think she's gonna nick us.

1ND KID. What get a copper?

3RD KID. She's gonna get a copper.

ALL KIDS. Oh Oh Oh.

3RD KID. (sings)

I went down the lane to buy a penny whistle
A copper took it off me and gimme a lump of gristle
I asked him for it back, he said he hadn't got it
(all) You lying git, you lying git, you got it in your
                                                    (pocket.
I wish I were a Bobby
Dressed up in Bobby's clothes
With a big tall hat
And a bellyful of fat
And a pancake in front for a nose.

MARGE. (near tears)
Please. Please don't. And please get in a straight line.

(Blows the whistle)

Don't you see...you've got to behave in school. If you

41

don't behave you'll grow up...bad. Little thugs.
Criminals, with black marks by your name.

(The KIDS chant)

KIDS.
Be a good girl, lead a good life.
Get a good husband, and be a good wife.

MARGE. (at once passionately) Fuck you, fuck you.

KIDS. Cor, cor, Miss is swearing. (They back away) She's
going mad. Miss is going mad. (They quietly huddle
into a group away from her. Then they go round and
fill up the windscreen)

Wonder what Miss Jill is going to do?

1ST KID. Go up the hill with Jack?

2ND KID. Go up the hill with Jack in a van?

3RD KID. My dad says loose women roam about the
countryside getting lifts from men, and are a menace.

2ND KID. My dad says summat like that, too.

4TH KID. An' my Dad says the whole country's sex-mad,
and they sex mad maniacs are all over the road in cars,
an' up the lanes, in lay-bys, and they should all have it
cut off, and Hitler was right, my Dad says.

KIDS. We're off, we're off, we're off in a motor car.
Sixty coppers are after us and they don't know where we
are.

(They disappear, all ducking down at once. The lights
come up to full again. Immediately, background of
motorway noises which continue throughout the next
episode. JACK and MARGE get the table and stand it in
midstage as a motorway bridge. JACK has binoculars)

JACK. Bloody marvellous. That girl's had five standing
arrangements in that lorry park in the last half hour.

42

MARGE. Are you going to be here all day?

JACK. Sssssh.

MARGE. I said are you going to be here -

JACK. All right. You go ahead.

MARGE. Let's go and have tea. We've been out here for hours. I'm dying for a tea.

JACK. I'm concentrating. (To the road) Say No.

MARGE. What d'you mean?

JACK. Say no.

MARGE. I'm not well.

JACK. You're not well.

MARGE. I'm not. Jack. Jack, I'm pregnant. I was sick this morning. I've been trying to tell you for the last half hour.

JACK. It's not possible.

MARGE. There isn't anybody else.

JACK. I should hope not.

MARGE. There isn't.

JACK. Right.

(Road noise envelops again, and they gesture. Then diminuendo)

MARGE. I sent it off Thursday. I got result in the post today.

JACK. One of those two quid jobs?

MARGE. I'm pregnant.

JACK. Ah.

MARGE. I don't know whether to have it or not.

JACK. You got five.

MARGE. It's not the same. I can't go through with it again.

JACK. It's all right.

MARGE. We can't talk here. I'm pregnant, Jack. I want to talk to you about it.

JACK. There's not much I can say. When I was a kid I used to come shooting rabbits round here. I saw some rabbits today. They got used to the noise. (On binoculars) There they are. Hallo, they've just picked up one of the girls on the slip road. On the go.

MARGE. The police have been. About the girl.

JACK. Well? I didn't knock her up. It was in her mouth.

MARGE. She said to stop it when you beat her. She's reported you to the police. She said it was rape.

JACK. Police have got their hands full. She came down on me. She knew what it was about. Tough as old boots.

MARGE. (casual) She's changed her mind.

(JACK resumes watching through binoculars. Pause. He panics inaudibly)

What?

JACK. Shit. Look. (Gives her binoculars) What they doing in the car park?

MARGE. Who? (Police appear in the van window)

JACK. That's mine. That's my fucking van. They're breaking into my fucking van.

44

MARGE. They've got the mattress out.

JACK. They're knocking it off.

MARGE. But it's the police.

JACK. You're right. Right. Shit. Shit.

(Police come on and handcuff them. They sit down at each
end of the table. The motorway noise ends suddenly.
They are turned away. Have difficulty in talking to each
other. Furtive. Fast)

Sorry about this. My alibi fell through.

MARGE. They arrested me at the school.

JACK. Sorry about that. I told them I wasn't there. I
told her I was in Bolton.

MARGE. Why bring me into it? I was at school in front of
the class.

JACK. It'll be all right. I think I got it worked out.

MARGE. You told them I was there.

JACK. Well I had to.

MARGE. What d'you mean?

JACK. I had to tell them.

MARGE. Not me.

JACK. I had to tell. I got it all worked out -

MARGE. I've been charged.

JACK. Look they know I was there. They know you were
there.

MARGE. But why did you tell them?

JACK. I told you. My alibi fell through. I had to tell them something.

MARGE. Not about me.

JACK. I had to tell them a bit of it. You were there and nothing happened.

MARGE. I wasn't watching.

JACK. Look nothing -

MARGE. I was looking out the front.

JACK. They won't believe that.

MARGE. I gave a statement.

JACK. Did you have a lawyer?

MARGE. They said I'd be all right if I said I wasn't in with it.

JACK. They'll never believe it.

MARGE. I asked you to take me home.

JACK. Ah, come on.

MARGE. That's what I said.

JACK. They won't believe it.

MARGE. They took it down.

JACK. They'll have you for aiding and abetting.

MARGE. But I wasn't.

JACK. You'll get three years.

MARGE. I've got five kids.

JACK. Doesn't mean a thing.

46

MARGE. I didn't do anything. I didn't look.

JACK. Tell that to the marines. Say what I say.

MARGE. But it's the truth.

JACK. If you say I was doing the girl then we both get
hit. If you say I wasn't doing anything, then we're both
in the clear.

MARGE. I don't see that.

JACK. What are you going to say?

MARGE. I didn't see anything.

JACK. They'll still get you. You got to back me up.

MARGE. But it's not true.

JACK. Nor's yours.

MARGE. I'll lose my job.

JACK. All right. I'll tell you what it was.

MARGE. I can't get involved.

JACK. It was heavy petting.

MARGE. I didn't see.

JACK. That's not good enough. The girl's unreliable.

MARGE. You should have been careful.

JACK. I was careful. I didn't put her up the spout.

MARGE. No - picking up hitchers.

JACK. I thought she wanted it. She acted like it.

MARGE. Aiding and abetting rape.

JACK. Heavy petting. What she said won't stand up in court. She's a junkie. Unreliable.

MARGE. You should have been more careful.

JACK. I don't do it with anyone unless they want.

MARGE. You've done it this time.

JACK. Not if we're careful. Remember. Only heavy petting. Only.

(POLICE take them off. Telephone exchange noises. Bells, lines engaged etc., BARBER's voice and another voice. LESLEY comes on and sits on the table. She gets out syringe, spoon. Melts up some heroin in a spoon over a match, draws it up into the syringe. She ties a rubber tube round her arm above the elbow and injects a vein. She finishes, tucks the tube into her trousers, exits as the speeches end)

VOICE 1. Hello - (Sound of crossed line) Hello, Barber here.

VOICE 2. Hello -

VOICE 1. The girl lied. She wasn't raped. She was quite willing.

She perjured. There was some pressure on her to - the police thought it was cut and dried.

Corker got eight years for rape, two years for indecent assault, the sentences to run concurrently.

She perjured.

VOICE 2. Ah.

VOICE 1. The girl. I feel I ought to raise the matter -

VOICE 2. Of course. It's rather unsavoury. I'm surprised in that sense.

JACK: James Warrior.  POLICEMAN: Graham Simpson.

JACK.  Heavy petting.  What she said won't stand up in
   court.  She's a junkie.  Unreliable.

VOICE 1. I think I ought to take it on myself.

VOICE 2. You're your own master.

VOICE 1. It's cut and dried. Ten years for the man, in prison. But the girl lied you see, she lied. She consented. It was her mother, when she saw the cane marks made her go. There are photographs of her doing this with men in the fields. On sale in London bookstores. Colour. £4 the set. There's no doubt about her complicity. I've got a letter here (Sounds of paper) I'll read it out.

VOICE 2. If you must.

VOICE 1. (louder) She is lying, she does that all the time with men, for money and sometimes not, also she is on drugs, double dex and meth that night she said, she is a liar, she did it willingly and she is always doing that thing, I took photos out of her bag when she was in the ladies with me, in a field with a man's object in her mouth. She does it all the time ever since I knowed her.

VOICE 2. Sounds like the genuine article. But you're wasting your time. It's hardly a cause.

VOICE 1. It matters that there has been a wrongful imprisonment for rape.

VOICE 2. A man that has young girls suck him off then beats them in the back of vans...hardly a saint.

VOICE 1. And the man's mistress was sentenced to three years, three years for aiding and abetting the rape.

VOICE 3. (WOMAN's voice) She goes to Holloway. He goes to Brixton. Her van goes off through Covent Garden up through Camden Town and out onto the Finchley Road. His wagon passes across Waterloo Bridge, Nine Elms and the Wandsworth Road.

(Ambulance bells)

And then they find she's pregnant, see, pregnant lady in

LESLEY: Catherine Kessler.

VOICE 1. ...also she is on drugs, double dex and meth
that night she said...

prison, doesn't give the infant a good start in life, fucking barbaric in fact, happens all the time. Unfair. Anyhow there's this kid, growing in her womb all the time, science tells us they feel the tension, I mean the great heartbeat revs up, the umbilicus twitches, the placenta turns, and all on a diet of 1,800 calories a day and no redress for strange cravings. Anyhow there she is hoping the little bastard'll turn blue and suffocate in her blood or whatever, a fall on the stone steps maybe, as gin baths or quinine are out of the question, hoping against hope that the ovary's going to change its mind and float free of the womb walling, but no she's going to have it, plans to strangle it when it comes out, there's a law, mothers aren't culpable after birth, due to the balance of the mind being disturbed, anyhow they hold her down, and the labour pains start which she doesn't want and the kid comes out. It's a terrible mess, the kid's all right though. Ten toes and a brain, but they're brutes, they take it away and make her clear up the after birth, don't treat people better than animals...

VOICE 1. Barber here. It isn't right. I mean we can't ignore it can we. Not after what... (Pause) I said we couldn't ignore it. It's entirely technical, fellatio can't possibly be rape, not in the letter of the law, one is just being prudish... I don't want to leave this case just like that, I think that two years for indecent assault it all that the British judicial system is warranted in giving and the rest is witch hunting by people dazed by actions which they don't understand. However.

(The reception fades. LESLEY exits. DICK and DOUG come on. They are hospital orderlies. They bring on a sling to lift the bodies with, and two thick polythene aprons. They stack these and go and lean on the table)

ANNOUNCEMENT OVER SPEAKERS. (fuzzed recording) Orderly call to move organ trolley from number 3 operating theatre to refrigeration vaults, urgent. Orderly call to move organ trolley from number 3 operating theatre to refrigeration vaults, urgent.

DICK. Nothing in for half an hour.

DOUG. No.

(They yawn.)

DICK. Maybe they're not dropping down anymore.

DOUG. Go out and shoot one.

(They laugh halfheartedly. Stop. A pause)

POLICEMAN. (off) Oy.

DICK. 'ere we go. Stand by your beds.

(Takes a last drag on a fag. Stubs it out with his foot)

POLICEMAN. (off) Oy, Shop. (They go off) Found her lying in a lay by. Saw her legs in the headlights. Got her?

DICK. Hasn't been like this since you found it?

POLICEMAN. (off) Nice and quiet, Dick. Just like you like them.

DOUG. Bring it in then.

POLICEMAN. Pretty little thing.

(They bring LESLEY in on a stretcher. She is unconscious)

DICK. We grow accustomed to that. Number 2 cubicle?

DOUG. I should say number 2.

POLICEMAN. (off) Who's going to sign?

DOUG. Dick will do that. He's good at Dr. Grey's. Specialises in Dr. Grey's, don't you?

POLICEMAN. (off) Shouldn't the doctor, eh, himself...

DOUG. Please yourself. You'll be here all night...

(DICK goes off to sign, comes back)

POLICEMAN. (off) Night lads.

DOUG. Night.

DICK. Night.

DOUG. Not seen this one before. (He lifts an arm. Tut tuts) Knitting needles.

DICK. Ere.

DOUG. What?

DICK. The one from the carpark.

DOUG. What you on about?

DICK. Last Monday.

DOUG. Oh yeh.

(Pause. They look at each other)

Who's going to have a peep.

(Nods. DICK looks up her arse. Pokes two fingers in. Takes out a screwed up bit of baccy foil. Opens it and sniffs)

DICK. True to form.

DOUG. Right down the line.

DICK. Yeh.

DOUG. Really weird, isn't it. When you think about it.

(DOUG puts the hash in his pocket. Enter a DOCTOR)

DOCTOR. Thank you gentlemen.

54

(Begins an examination at once. DOUG and DICK behind him. Lifts the arm as DOUG did)

Patch of perforation marks, upper forelimb, left side.

(Lifts her right side)

Ditto right side.

(Looks a little closer briefly)

Septic.

(To her head. Lifts the lids, of left eye)

Dilated of course.

(Lifts other lid)

Ditto. No retinal movement.

(Now going down her body)

Nasal phalange, left side, inflamed. Some gum inflammation. Prominent halitosis. Tonsils degenerate. Obviously untreated dental caries. Lips suspect. Lower jaw. Acne there, skin scorched by self-treatment. Cervical glands. Yes. Yes. Ah yes. Query tuberculoid. Tertiary nipple in left armpit. Right armpit, some rashing, infected razor cut. Breasts good. Bladder distended. Colonic obstruction an informed guess. Some evidence of healed pudendic eruption. Active boil labia major. Yes. Some pururient vaginal discharge. Yes. Thighs. Further patches of perforation marks. Yes. Yes. Legs. Good. Good. Perforation mark in the heel of the right foot. Gentlemen.

(DICK and DOUG come forward and flip her over expertly then step back)

Elongated abrasions. Bruising. Certainly applied in some manner. On the calves, seven abrasions in figures of eight. On the thighs...

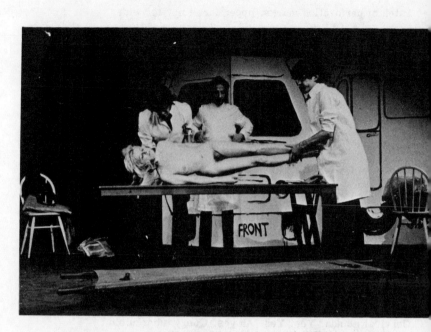

LESLEY: Catherine Kessler.  DOCTOR: Nicholas Nacht.
DICK: Mark York.  DOUG: Graham Simpson.

(DICK and DOUG come forward and flip her over expertly,
    then step back)

(He counts quickly)

3 abrasions in single furrows, evenly spaced. On the buttocks.

(He counts quickly)

Fifteen abrasions, some fading, in a gatelike pattern. Two heavy bruises, one with skin abrasion the other without.

(He runs his hand up her back)

Fine, fine.

(Stops. Traces an area with his fingers, between her shoulder blades)

Between the shoulder blades. Snowflake pattern, of heavy infection. Very deep. Telling, very telling. Thank you gentlemen.

(From his top pocket he takes a tag, writes something on it)

Tag her for me would you?

(He hands the tag to DICK and goes off. DICK and DOUG read the tag. Look at each other and shrug. They are tying the tag on LESLEY's big toe when the DOCTOR looks back in)

Eh, boys.

(They look up)

If Nurse Cunningham doesn't come, can you...

(Nods)

DICK. We're not nurses, Sir.

DOCTOR. Please yourself. If you want to be here all night.

(The DOCTOR goes off)

DICK. Oh well.

DOUG. Oh well.

DICK. We always get their crap. Doug. As you say. Wash
her.

DOUG. Yeh.

DICK. Yeh.

DOUG. So pretty, and yet so rancid.

DICK. What?

DOUG. Never mind.

DICK. She's a nice girl. Where's the sponge?

DOUG. In the bucket.

(DICK goes off. DOUG tips her nipples with his finger)

Bomp bomp, bomp bomp. Hello? Anyone in? Anyone in?

(Nothing from LESLEY. DICK comes back with the bucket
and sponge. He soaks the sponge)

Ere.

DOUG. What.

DICK. Not so fast.

(DOUG stops)

I mean, let's see what we can get.

(DOUG looks off right and left)

O.K.

58

(DOUG puts the bucket down)

DICK. Look Pedlos.

    (Picks up her legs. Pumps them back and forward)

    Pump, pump, pump, pump, eh?

DOUG. Yeh!

DICK. What do you fancy now?

DOUG. A bit of bumph I think.

DICK. Great!

    (At once they turn her on her back. DICK takes her
    wrists and DOUG takes her ankles. They lift her clear
    of the stretcher, and swing her)

    Oh look at her wobbles.

DOUG. Wobble wubble, wobble wubble, wobble wobble
    wobble, Eh?

DICK. Great.

DOUG. Great wobbles!

DICK. Wobble, wibble, woops!

    (They've dropped her. Pause. DICK bends over her.
    Looks her in the face. Her eyes have opened. Their
    conversation with her is normal and calm)

    Hello Miss.

LESLEY. What...

DICK. It's all right Miss. Just let us get you on the table
    Miss. Can you just give us a hand, Doug?

DOUG. Right-ho Dick.

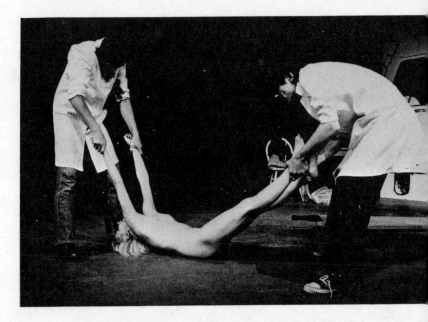

DICK: Mark York.   LESLEY: Catherine Kessler.
DOUG: Graham Simpson.

(At once they turn her on her back.  JACK takes her wrists
and DOUG takes her ankles.  They lift her clear of the
stretcher, and swing her)

LESLEY. But...

DOUG. Just keep limp Miss. We'll do the rest.

   (They lift her onto the table)

   There's nothing to get worried about. We're just getting
   you a blanket.

LESLEY. I, eh...

   (She covers her breasts)

DICK. Yeh, here we are.

   (Covers her with a blanket)

   Warm enough? Now Miss, you're in the Central Hospital,
   and the doctor asked me to tell you, there's nothing...

   (She interrupts)

LESLEY. What's that?

DICK. What's what?

LESLEY. That. On my foot.

DICK. Don't worry about that. That's just a reminder.

LESLEY. I don't...

DICK. What you've got to think of Miss, is that it's all
   right now.

LESLEY. I didn't...

DICK. Course not, Miss. (Very kind) You see, they can
   clear it up. Can't they, Doug?

DOUG. Yes Miss. They can smooth it all over, these days.
   That's what it's all about. Now look, we're just going to
   give you a bit of a wash, Miss.

LESLEY: Catherine Kessler.    DICK: Mark York.

DICK.   (Covers her with blanket)

LESLEY. Oh, I...

   (Writhing up. Trying to touch her back. Loudly)

   I'm not going to. It's more than you think, you don't
   know it's more than you think.

DICK. Just... (Then softly) Be quiet Miss. (They push her
   back. She lies still. A slow fade starts) You see, you're
   just waiting now. You're going to be attended to.

DOUG. And while you're waiting, we're going to wash you.
   That's all right, isn't it?

DICK. Don't want to be all mucky for the doctor, do you?

DOUG. If your Mum and Dad come in, you've got a mum
   and dad? Well your mum and dad will want to see you
   clean.

   (They get the sponge and bucket up onto the table. They
   both put gloves on)

DICK. It's wonderful. What they're going to do for you.
   What's going to happen to you. Isn't it, Doug?

DOUG. The way you came in, and the way you'll go out.
   It's a miracle, when you think of it.

DICK. A lot of trouble, a lot of care, Miss. All along the
   line.

LESLEY. No, no, don't do that...

DICK. It's just warm water, Miss.

   (LESLEY dies. They put the aprons on as they read the
   tag on her toe. Then DOUG gets a monster three
   wheeled dustbin out)

DOUG. In the event of death the nurse should be informed
   first. If the nurse is not available, the informant should
   go to the doctor or surgeon. If there is no person in
   authority, then the informant shall wash the body and lay

63

out the limbs in an accepted, dignified position before rigor mortis sets in.

DICK. An accepted dignified position.

DOUG. That's what the man said.

(The bucket has got blood in it. They wash the body in blood and put it in the sling. They hoist the body up with a pulley and lower it into the bin)

Makes you philosophical. (DICK lights a fag) Take mice.

DICK. You tell me.

DOUG. So they put these perfectly normal mice in this cage see? And they leave them. Just feed 'em and leave 'em. And they multiply and die and multiply and some more die. And the number grows. And grows. And there isn't enough room any more. They can't turn round. Take proper exercise. Tripping over each other's shit. And then it all starts to fall apart. Anarchy, chaos. Total irreversible breakdown. Nothing. Void. The whole thing.

DICK. We're not animals.

DOUG. I dunno. I sometimes catch myself sniffing around. If you get my drift.

DICK. Human beings have superhuman potential. Man can rise. He's got the wings. But they're rusty.

DOUG. I've heard it all.

DICK. Well that's typical.

DOUG. That's right.

DICK. All right. I can't argue with you, can I?

DOUG. Yeah.

DICK. You won't listen.

64

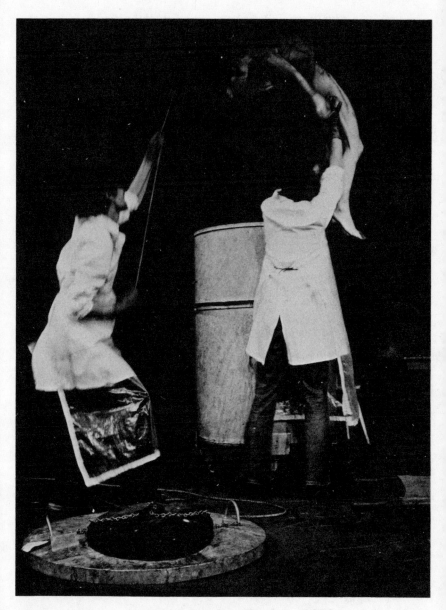

DICK: Mark York.   LESLEY: Catherine Kessler.   DOUG:
Graham Simpson.

(DOUG and DICK wash the body in blood.  They hoist the
body up with a pulley and lower it into the bin)

DOUG. I will.

DICK. Your mind's full of snot.

   (They go off with the stretcher and bring on the body of
   JACK, naked. They wash it in blood, put it in the sling
   and hoist it into the bin)

DOUG. The problem is too many fucking people.

DICK. Far too many.

DOUG. That's the problem. There ought to be incentives.

DICK. Cash you mean?

DOUG. Handouts.

DICK. Or castration.

DOUG. That as well. Regiments of sterilisers, driving
   all over in landrovers. Keeping a close watch.

DICK. I think it's certain that either we lick the population
   question or it's World War Three.

DOUG. Certainly. That's where we can agree. We gonna
   tear each other apart. Less someone does something
   serious about it. Like (Pause) dropping ten H bombs on
   Red China.

DICK. You got to do something when you get down to it.

   (Pause)

   I mean what are we doing here? Doug?

DOUG. (shrugs) I dunno.

   (They go off with the stretcher and bring on the naked
   body of MARGE. They wash it in blood, hoist it in the
   bin)

DICK. There's some fucking mysterious purpose in this

66

fucking mysterious life. And I'm determined to get at
it. Winkle it out.

DOUG. We all got that urge.

DICK. That's what makes us human beings. Doug, I'm
going to find it, do you hear me? Can you hear me, Doug?
I'm going to keep going because that's all I can do.
And someday maybe we're going to know what it's all
about. Maybe not in my lifetime - Christ, Doug, I'm
getting on - maybe not in my kids' or my kids' kids',
but some day some man's goin' to tear the universe apart,
say this is what it means, this is what it's meant all
along, and back there - back along there are millions
of people, and they did the spadework, they never knew,
but it's because of them and their suffering, it's because
they've suffered and lived, Doug, because we've lived,
it's because of us, because of our suffering that it's
all obvious now and what it all means.

(Pause)

My mum died last week.

DOUG. Oh yes.

DICK. She went off round tea time.

DOUG. Old, was she?

DICK. Not particularly. She was religious. She said she
didn't mind the pain.

DOUG. What did she die of?

DICK. Melanoblastoma. The doctor wanted to give her this
stuff. Mixture of morphine and gin. Best thing in the
world for the old dear to be blotto, couldn't stand the
screams, what was left of her vocal cords. They put
her in a home.

DOUG. That's fair.

DICK. I mean, Christ, Doug, I mean shit -

DOUG. Yeah.

DICK. (meaning MARGE) I mean. Look at this one. We'll
all get our balls chewed for this. When she goes. I
mean it's another dead junkie. Who cares? Jesus.
This country's got three hundred thousand full time
lushes. There's eighty thousand a year dying from self-
induced lung-cancer. There's thousands on the roads.
This one chose to die of pox, drugs, general malnutrition
in a free affluent society. She <u>chose</u>. But we'll get our
balls chewed off all the same.

(They collect two large churns of water and pour them
in the dustbin)

DOUG. That's a facile observation.

DICK. Yeah well.

(Pause)

I'm a facile sort of person.

DOUG. They don't choose to live in India. They starve.

DICK. I know. Don't shout. I know.

DOUG. Well they - do.

DICK. I know.

DOUG. Good. There you are then.

DICK. Yeah.

DOUG. Yeah.

DICK. It's a good thing I'm a friend of yours or I'd smash
your face in.

DOUG. Well. There you go.

(Pause)

I mean, just think about it. There're cows walking around, and men in the gutter dying of starvation but they won't eat the cows. It's not right.

(Pause)

Is it?

DICK. I don't think you should bring these subjects up.

DOUG. Why not? Why not? It's the major problem of the 20th Century, isn't it?

DICK. I just don't think you should bring it up.

DOUG. But it's important.

DICK. It's not right to bring it up!

DOUG. Don't you care then.

DICK. Course I care!

DOUG. You know what you are. Crystal.

DICK. What am I?

DOUG. Liberal scum.

(They put several shovel fulls of pips in the bin)

DICK. What's that then? I mean I know you're trying to insult me. I mean I know you're really scraping the barrel, really dredging it all up to insult your very good friend...

DOUG. Liberal scum is the lowest level of shit in our shitty society mate, so there.

DICK. Oh I see.

(Pause)

The lowest level in our shitty...

(Nods)

Yes. (Fiercely)

DICK. I think you are a bug eyed Pharisee. Yes. That's not bad. Yeah.

DOUG. They're dying out there. Tonight. Out there, dying. Their tummies are puffing up. Their navels are popping with gases. And what are you offering to the solution of mankind's agony? Petty personal abuse.

DICK. Well what are you offering then.

DOUG. At least I am offering.

(DOUG stirs it with a big broom handle)

(Stuck then...)

The depth of my human concern.

DICK. You're joking.

DOUG. I don't joke about that!

DICK. The depth of your human concern? I saw you stub a fag out on a patient's arse, not two weeks ago.

DOUG. Well.

DICK. Well what?

DOUG. Just... Well.

DICK. I do wish we could have a rational argument. Without you picking on me.

DOUG. You are a grubby little man, sometimes.

DICK. There! There you go!

DOUG. They're starving... Bellies... (Together) Puffing up navels popping.

DOUG. Well they are. They are.

DICK. All right. All right.

DOUG. Arms like matchsticks.

DICK. All right. All right.

DOUG. Eyes with cataracts. Beri beri. Little children.

DICK. All right.

(DOUG goes up and takes off his rubber gloves, dips his hand in the bin and brings it out with a big gob of jam on it. They sit down and share it)

You've won your argument.

DOUG. I should think so.

DICK. I waive all rights of reply. O.K.? You're right.

DOUG. Right.

DICK. It's an intellectual privilege. Changing your mind.

DOUG. Ho. Ho.

DICK. Nothing to be ashamed of.

DOUG. No.

DICK. It's a waste of time. Gods aren't ashamed.

DOUG. Neither are mice.

(The lights fade rapidly)

DICK. You could have stirred it up a bit more.

# C AND B PLAYSCRIPTS

|  | Cloth | Paper |
|---|---|---|
| *PS11 THE WITNESSES and other plays (The Old Woman Broods, The Funny Old Man) Tadeusz Rozewicz tr. Adam Czerniawski | £1.50 | 60p |
| *PS 12 THE CENCI Antonin Artaud tr. Simon Watson Taylor | 90p | 40p |
| *PS 13 PRINCESS IVONA Witold Gombrowicz tr. Krystyna Griffith-Jones and Catherine Robins | £1.05 | 45p |
| *PS 14 WIND IN THE BRANCHES OF THE SASSAFRAS René de Obaldia tr. Joseph Foster | £1.25 | 45p |
| *PS 15 INSIDE OUT and other plays (Still Fires, Rolley's Grave) Jan Quackenbush | £1.05 | 45p |
| *PS 16 THE SWALLOWS Roland Dubillard tr. Barbara Wright | £1.25 | 55p |
| PS 17 THE DUST OF SUNS Raymond Roussel | £1.50 | 60p |
| PS 18 EARLY MORNING Edward Bond | £1.25 | 55p |
| PS 19 THE HYPOCRITE Robert McLellan | £1.25 | 50p |
| PS 20 THE BALACHITES and THE STRANGE CASE OF MARTIN RICHTER Stanley Eveling | £1.50 | 60p |

|  |  | Cloth | Paper |
|---|---|---|---|
| *PS 31 | STRINDBERG<br>Colin Wilson | £1.05 | 45p |
| *PS 32 | THE FOUR LITTLE GIRLS<br>Pablo Picasso<br>tr. Roland Penrose | £1.25 | 50p |
| PS 33 | MACRUNE'S GUEVARA<br>John Spurling | £1.25 | 45p |
| *PS 34 | THE MARRIAGE<br>Witold Gombrowicz<br>Tr. Louis Iribarne | £1.75 | 75p |
| *PS 35 | BLACK OPERA and THE GIRL<br>WHO BARKS LIKE A DOG<br>Gabriel Cousin<br>tr. Irving F. Lycett | £1.50 | 75p |
| *PS 36 | SAWNEY BEAN<br>Robert Nye and Bill Watson | £1.25 | 50p |
| PS 37 | COME AND BE KILLED and DEAR JANET<br>ROSENBERG, DEAR MR. KOONING<br>Stanley Eveling | £1.75 | 75p |
| PS 38 | DISCOURSE ON VIETNAM<br>Peter Weiss<br>tr. Geoffrey Skelton | £1.90 | 90p |
| *PS 39 | ! HEIMSKRINGLA ! or THE STONED<br>ANGELS<br>Paul Foster | £1.50 | 60p |
| *PS 41 | THE HOUSE OF BONES<br>Roland Dubillard<br>tr. Barbara Wright | £1.75 | 75p |
| *PS 42 | THE TREADWHEEL and COIL<br>WITHOUT DREAMS<br>Vivienne C. Welburn | £1.75 | 75p |

|  |  | Cloth | Paper |
|---|---|---|---|
| PS 43 | THE NUNS<br>Eduardo Manet<br>tr. Robert Baldick | £1.25 | 50p |
| PS 44 | THE SLEEPERS DEN and OVER<br>GARDENS OUT<br>Peter Gill | £1.25 | 50p |
| PS 45 | A MACBETH<br>Charles Marowitz | £1.50 | 75p |
| PS 46 | SLEUTH<br>Anthony Shaffer | £1.25 | 60p |
| *PS47 | SAMSON and ALISON MARY FAGAN<br>David Selbourne | £1.25 | 60p |
| *PS 48 | OPERETTA<br>Witold Gombrowicz<br>tr. Louis Iribarne | £1.60 | 65p |
| *PS 49 | THE NUTTERS and other plays<br>(Social Service, A Cure for Souls)<br>A.F. Cotterell | £1.65 | 75p |
| PS 50 | THE GYMNASIUM and other plays<br>(The Technicians, Stay Where You Are,<br>Jack the Giant-Killer, Neither Here Nor There)<br>Olwen Wymark | £1.60 | 75p |
| PS 51 | THE MAN IN THE GREEN MUFFLER<br>and other plays (In Transit, The Sword)<br>Stewart Conn | £1.50 | 60p |
| *PS 52 | CALCIUM and other plays<br>(Coins, Broken, The Good Shine, Victims)<br>Jan Quackenbush | £1.80 | 95p |
| *PS 53 | FOUR BLACK REVOLUTIONARY PLAYS<br>(Experimental Death Unit 1, A Black Mass,<br>Great Goodness of Life, Madheart)<br>Leroi Jones | £1.25 | 55p |

| | | Cloth | Paper |
|---|---|---|---|
| PS 54 | LONG VOYAGE OUT OF WAR<br>Ian Curteis | £2.25 | £1.05 |
| PS 55 | INUIT and THE OTHERS<br>David Mowat | £1.75 | 75p |
| PS 56 | ALL CHANGE and other plays<br>(Party For Six, Magic Afternoon)<br>Wolfgang Bauer<br>tr. Martin & Renata Esslin,<br>Herb Greer | £1.95 | 95p |
| PS 57 | CURTAINS<br>Tom Mallin | £1.60 | 70p |
| PS 58 | VAGINA REX AND THE GAS OVEN<br>Jane Arden | £1.25 | 55p |
| *PS 59 | SLAUGHTER NIGHT and other plays<br>Roger Howard | £1.50 | 60p |
| PS 60 | AS TIME GOES BY and BLACK PIECES<br>Mustapha Matura | £2.25 | £1.00 |
| PS 61 | MISTER and OH STARLINGS!<br>Stanley Eveling | £1.75 | 75p |
| PS 62 | OCCUPATIONS and THE BIG HOUSE<br>Trevor Griffiths | £2.50 | £1.00 |
| *PS 64 | MR. JOYCE IS LEAVING PARIS<br>Tom Gallacher | £1.95 | 95p |
| PS 65 | IN THE HEART OF THE BRITISH MUSEUM<br>John Spurling | £1.95 | 95p |

*All plays marked thus are represented for dramatic
presentation by:
C and B (Theatre) Ltd, 18 Brewer Street, London W1